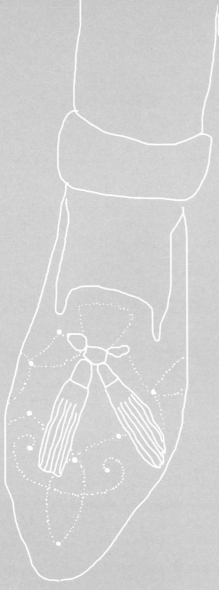

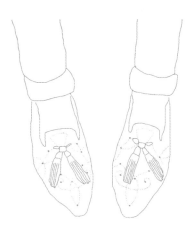

En Brogue

En Brogue

Love Fashion.
Love Shoes.
Hate Heels.

HANNAH ROCHELL

SALT·YARD BOOK Co.

This book is for anyone who's ever taken their heels off on the dance floor at a wedding, lugged about emergency flat shoes in their handbag, or fallen down a set of steps in a pair of platforms.

Contents

Introduction

EnBrogue.com is a blog about stylish flat shoes written by me – Hannah Rochell – a fashion editor who never wears heels. I'd never felt comfortable in heels, but when I embarked on a career in fashion I felt a certain pressure to wear them. As a result, I totally lost my style identity (I'm a bit of a tomboy) and I fell over. A lot.

I remember the exact moment I decided to get rid of the few pairs of heels I did own. It had been raining, and I was running for a train at Waterloo station in a pair of Pierre Hardy for Gap green suede, sheepskin-lined platform boots. I took a bad tumble on the slippery floor and a girl came to my rescue shouting, 'Oh no! You fell over in your lovely Gap boots!' No boots are lovely enough to make that much of a spectacle of yourself for. Not to mention the fact that I'd really hurt my knee. The heels had to go, so I gave them all away to friends and charity shops.

It's a very liberating thing, knowing you're not going to fall over in public. Only wearing flats means I can dance all night at weddings (I've worn flats as a bridesmaid, even though I'm 5'3" and the other two bridesmaids were just shy of 6 foot). I can walk up the escalators if I am in a hurry or approach a set of steep steps with confidence. I never have to buy those squidgy pads to prevent my feet from aching, because all my shoes are comfortable. And best of all, my part sixties mod, part Britpop tomboy wardrobe makes sense again.

> I firmly believe that just because a shoe doesn't have a killer heel, it doesn't mean that it can't be beautiful. For me, wearing flat shoes is a comfortable and stylish option. It's a win win situation.

EnBrogue.com came about after I was posting pictures of the flat shoes I was wearing to London Fashion Week

on Instagram. They were a hit – turns out there are a lot of people out there who like to talk about comfortable footwear. I've been blogging, illustrating and generally talking non-stop on the subject ever since. So if you're like me and you love fashion but hate heels, I think you'll love this book too – a celebration of stylish flat shoes.

Hannah is features editor at fashion magazine InStyle *and has over seven years' experience as a fashion journalist. EnBrogue.com has been featured on BBC Radio 4's* Saturday Live *programme, in the* Observer *weekend magazine,* The Times, The Saturday Times *magazine,* Red Online *and* Look.co.uk.

Ankle straps

What, you might ask, is there to say about this shoe other than the fact that there is a strap around the ankle? Well, not an awful lot I suppose, but I love this style of pointy pump; it's really flattering, bizarrely managing to lengthen the legs when it ought, really, to do the exact opposite. Ankle boots can make legs look shorter, whereas ankle straps still show off most of your foot, with much more flattering results.

There's something a little nostalgic about these shoes, too. They're like a much sexier version of the Mary Janes you might have worn at school, particularly if you avoid dark colours like black and navy, which might look like actual school shoes. To that end, I like to style my white pair in a bit of a retro vibe – the dress I'm wearing here was made by my mum in the late 1960s.

Kurt Geiger shoes

Ballet pumps

Back in the early noughties, one style of shoe suddenly liberated women who were fed up with heels but wanted something more feminine than lace-ups. That shoe was the ballet pump, popularised by Kate Moss, who wore them every day for what seemed like three years straight with skinny jeans (another phenomenon we didn't realise we needed in our lives) and simple, loose-fitting tops.

> To prevent yourself from looking like you are en route to an 8th birthday party, the key is to choose pumps that are a narrow fit and low cut on the foot, ideally with a bit of toe cleavage. French Sole (Moss's favourite) has nailed the most flattering cut of shoe; they make your legs look (almost) as long and elegant as a heel does.

French Sole pumps

There are so many examples, particularly where boots are concerned, of styles originally designed purely for practical purposes that happen also to look so cool that they end up being worn by people who have no interest whatsoever in the thing that they were designed for. For example, I have never been on a motorbike (well, I have once, but don't tell my mum – she'd kill me) but I've owned a few pairs of biker boots in my time.

> This style of boot has many important bike-related features, like the barely-there heel (for operating the pedal) and the fact that they are tall on the leg (to protect from the exhaust). That's all well and good, but I just reckon they look dead nice.

Lucy Choi London biker boots

Biker boots

Blucher boots

Blucher boots have a strong association with the armed forces. They replaced buckled boots during the Napoleonic wars and were standard issue in the Crimean War and the First Boer War and, as such, are also referred to as combat boots or army boots. Confusingly, in the US Derby lace-up shoes are commonly known as bluchers, too.

As well as laces, bluchers often have a side zip, which saves you having to unlace them every time you put them on and take them off. Handy. It also allows for some nifty styling, like wearing them laced-up but unzipped with baggy jeans tucked into them. Never wear with army combat trousers though! That would be a step too far.

Steve Madden 'Troopa' boots

Many people have taken to referring to all flat lace-up shoes as brogues. In fact, the term 'broguing' refers to the holes punched into the leather from which the shoes are constructed. This means you can have slip-on or even heeled brogues – they don't have to be flat lace-ups but they must have the holes.

Now we've cleared up that technicality, what are the holes for? Brogues (derived from the Gaelic word bróg, meaning 'shoe') were originally a country shoe worn by the Scottish and Irish when they needed to cross a bog. The holes allowed the water to drain out and the shoe to dry once it was taken off. Clever, eh? They looked so nice, though, that they were later adopted on formal shoes and are most commonly found on Derby, Oxford and monk styles.

Grenson 'Emily' brogues

Brogues

adidas Stan Smith

In 1972, an American tennis player called Stanley Roger Smith won Wimbledon wearing a pair of adidas 'Robert Haillet' tennis shoes. Their namesake was a French tennis player, but unfortunately for him, he never won a grand slam and Stan Smith was a much catchier name; a detail not lost on adidas, who renamed the shoe in Smith's honour after his success at the south London tournament.

It's no wonder that this humble white shoe is the best-selling tennis shoe of all time, with over 40 million pairs sold. Its simple design not only looks really smart on court – particularly when paired with Wimbledon whites – but it effortlessly makes the leap from sport to fashion and street style. I think its success lies in the minimalist design; the adidas 3-Stripes are just air holes in three neat lines, and there is usually only one accent colour (which, in my book, should always be classic green), making them easy to integrate into any type of wardrobe. Hip hop sportswear? Tick. Pinstripe trouser suit? Tick. Pencil skirt and cashmere sweater? Triple tick. No wonder they're favourites of everyone from David Bowie to Pharrell Williams.

Chelsea boots

Chelsea boots are a Victorian invention and were originally worn for horse riding. You can see why; those elastic 'gusset' sides make them easy to pull on and off, and who wants to mess with laces when there's mud and horse poo involved? A form of tall, pointy Chelsea boot was worn and popularised by The Beatles in the sixties, but, cool as they were, they had a Cuban heel so they're not a style you will find in my wardrobe! I prefer mine to be completely flat.

These days, you'll find all sorts of styles of Chelsea boot – pointed or round-toed, tall or short, with or without broguing – and I think they're one of the most useful smart styles of flat shoe you can have in your wardrobe.

DUO Chelsea boots

Chukkas are also known as desert boots, and usually have just two or three pairs of lace holes. They are often made of suede, though leather versions are a more practical option unless you're a dab hand with protective spray and a suede brush. (Incidentally, suede brushes really do work! Unless what you're trying to clean off your blue suede shoes is a kebab after a stag do, as Mr Brogue recently attempted.)

While the most famous makers of this style of boot are Clarks, you'll find countless other brands putting their own spin on this classic shoe. Skateboarding experts Vans have a style of chukka that looks more like a high-top trainer, and I love this pair by Swear with their modern elongated toe.

Swear boots

Chukkas

There's only one type of cowboy boot that fits in with the EnBrogue aesthetic. Western boots, which come up to just below the knee, have a pointed toe (to slip easily into the stirrup) and a Cuban heel of at least one inch in height (so that the foot stays put once in the stirrup); that's one inch too many for me! I prefer the roper style; it's a shorter boot, coming in at low calf height, and the heel is either flat or just ½ an inch, which is acceptable!

The best place to get cowboy boots is in vintage stores. They're usually extremely good quality and ready worn-in, so much more comfortable than a new pair. I'd advise wearing with anything but jeans (you don't want anyone to shout 'yee-haw!' at you in the street) and instead go for something more feminine, like a floral tea dress.

Vintage roper boots

Cowboy boots

Creepers

The creeper has its origins in North Africa during
World War II. It has a distinctive stacked crêpe sole,
and made its way into different subcultures to its
cousin, the desert boot – also developed in World War II
– once its veteran owners found their way home.

The first wave of creepers were worn by the Teddy Boys
of the 1950s, who teamed them with their distinctive
glossy quiffs and cropped trouser suits. They were later
adopted by punks and rockers in the seventies when
Malcolm McLaren and Vivienne Westwood began
selling them in their legendary shop on the Kings Road
in London. They were even Bananarama's footwear of
choice in the eighties, and have recently had a bit of
a renaissance (Rihanna loves them). These are made
by the original creeper designer, George Cox. Just add
a guitar.

Fred Perry Laurel Wreath George Cox Creepers

Deck shoes – also known as boat shoes and topsiders – are shoes designed for the sailing community that have made their way into mainstream fashion. The sailing thing comes from Paul Sperry, founder of shoe company Sperry Top-Siders, who invented them for purpose in 1935. Their oiled leather uppers are waterproof and the rubber soles are non-skid; perfect for dealing with the slippery surface of a yacht.

Timberland released its first deck shoes in 1979, and is the brand I associate strongest with this style of shoe. Although their most iconic style is the classic brown leather, they look great in navy with a flash of colour on the sole. Important styling tip: they should never be worn with socks!

Timberland deck shoes

Deck shoes

Birkenstocks

Although the Birkenstock family were making shoes in Germany as early as 1774, the sandals as we know them today didn't make an appearance until nearly two hundred years later. In 1964, Karl Birkenstock produced a prototype shoe including a flexible arch support, et voilà! The Marmite of all shoe styles was born.

Love them or hate them, Birks are good for you; those contoured cork and rubber soles actually mould to fit your feet. If you've ever had a pair, you'll know that this makes them feel odd at first – uncomfortable, even – but it's worth persevering. Their reputation hasn't always been that cool, but Birkenstocks have recently come back into favour in the fashion world, following some very expensive copycat versions finding their way down the catwalk at Paris Fashion Week. My favourite style is the Arizona (shown here), which was first introduced in 1973. My mum, on the other hand, prefers thong styles (debuted in 1982) and has five pairs! But then, once you've worn them in, there's nothing more comfortable in the world.

Derbys are a type of formal lace-up shoe, often confused with Oxfords. Well, they do look pretty similar. To distinguish between the two, we need to look at the vamp – the front section of the shoe – and the laces. A Derby, sometimes referred to as an open front shoe, has the lace holes on two obvious leather tabs that are stitched on top of the vamp, meaning you can open the shoe much wider than an Oxford. That also makes them really comfortable and easier to put on and take off.

Derbys can come in all shapes and sizes, with or without broguing. Here, Mr Brogue is sporting a rather handsome style with subtle brogue detailing and a removable fringe. I'm wearing a pair with cut-out details; perfect for breezy feet in the summer.

Hannah in Clarks 'Hotel Image'
Mr Brogue in Clarks 'Darby Desert'

Derbys

Espadrilles

My favourite place to buy espadrilles is any bog-standard French supermarket. I like to pick up a new pair each year for €5 or less when I'm shopping for baguettes and cheap wine (if I happen to be in Brittany, I'll pick up a cheap Breton stripe top for €8 while I'm there, too). A shoe designer recently told me that you are meant to throw your espadrilles away at the end of each summer, so I prefer not to spend too much money on them! And they're perfectly good quality, too, these French hypermarché shoes.

> That's because the French invented the espadrilles in the Pyrenees (with a bit of help from the Spanish – the word espadrille is derived from the Catalan esparto, the tough Mediterranean grass used for making the rope soles), so they know what they're doing. Wear with cropped cigarette trousers for 1940s chic.

French €5 espadrilles

Flip-flops

The most onomatopoeic of shoes – flip, flop, flip, flop
as you walk – are also one of the most popular around
the world. The modern rubber ones we know today
originate from the Japanese version called 'zōri' brought
back to the USA by soldiers returning from World War
II. Other name variations include 'thongs' in Australia
and, my favourite, 'jandals' – short for Japanese sandals
– in New Zealand.

> It's really bad for your feet to walk any sort of distance
> in flip-flops, and they're utterly unsuitable as city attire
> as you end up with filthy black feet by the end of the
> day. Personally, I reserve them for their natural habitat:
> the beach.

Flip-flops

The technical term for these shoes is kilties, and that dandy fringe was developed as a way of protecting your shoes on the golf course. Usually, the fringe will cover the laces to stop them getting wet on the dewy grass, but you'll also see it purely as a form of decoration, as on these delightful monks.

> I think some men find kilties a bit O.T.T., but they work brilliantly for women – we can get away with more flamboyant shoes! I'd even sanction wearing them with something crazy, like tartan trousers (I have done this), but maybe steer clear of Argyle socks and a flat cap.

Toast fringed monks

Fringed shoes

The term 'geek shoes' is a relatively recent one. In the last couple of years, 'geek chic' has become mainstream, with trendy young folk like my teenage nieces embracing dark-rimmed spectacles (even when they have perfect eyesight), knee-high socks and other attire you might have been teased about at school, such as sensible looking shoes.

It's the very fact that these shoes are sensible that makes me love them so much. They have the ventilation of a sandal but with an enclosed toe (safety first!) and two of my favourite ever shoe features: a T-bar and a crêpe sole. You can't beat them for comfort. If I'm feeling particularly geeky, I might pair them with my Blue Peter badge – proof that I was a real bona fide square when I was younger!

Y.M.C. 'Punk' sandal

Geek shoes

Clarks Originals Desert Boots

Clarks Originals Desert Boots were launched in 1950, but their concept dates back to 1944. They were designed by Nathan Clark (a member of that Clarks family), who was an army officer. He was inspired by the chukka boots made in the bazaars of Cairo that had been adopted as a practical option by the Eighth Army, who were transferred from North Africa to the Far East, where Clark was also stationed. Initially, Clarks weren't sure the design would sell, but after editorial coverage in the US edition of *Esquire* magazine in 1950 the shoe took off, at first in America and later in Europe.

> The distinctive features of a Clarks Originals Desert Boot are the crêpe sole (my favourite type of sole – so comfortable) and just four lace holes – two on either side. Strongly associated with mod culture in the UK, they are an absolute design classic, and are always in style. Most men I know own or have owned a pair, but I think they look brilliant on smaller feet (i.e. mine) teamed with a skirt or shorts in the summer. Just make sure your other half isn't wearing an identical pair or someone will have to get changed...

High-tops

These tall trainers originate from sports like baseball (Converse All Stars) and basketball (Nike Air Force 1) and, to be classed as a high-top, must extend above the ankle; there is also such a thing as a mid-top boot, which is slightly shorter.

> High-tops can be quite tricky to wear, particularly with jeans (a slim fit and turn-ups are essential!) but look great with short skirts. Getting it right is all about proportion. I prefer the slimmer baseball styles because I find they look more flattering on my little legs, but if you're taller, chunkier basketball styles look wonderful on your long legs.

Nike high-tops

I spent a lot of my youth at dance classes, which means I wore jazz shoes A LOT. In dance circles, we had our 'proper' jazz shoes for dancing in, with a soft suede sole, and our 'kick about' jazz shoes, which had a rubber sole suitable for wearing outdoors. I remember my first pair vividly – hand-me-downs from an older girl – they were white and quite grubby and too big but I loved them all the same.

Essentially, jazz shoes are very soft Oxford lace-ups. The flexible sole is a must-have feature and makes them more comfortable than a traditional dress shoe. They look great – and less dancer-y – in a bright, vivid colour.

Labour of Love jazz shoes

Jazz shoes

One of the first pairs of fashion shoes I remember owning was a pair of jellies in the mid 1980s. As I spent much of my childhood swimming in the sea, I'd already had plenty of jellies that looked like this, but the fashion pair were a more grown-up, slip-on style. I felt so cool in them, particularly when carrying my matching jelly bag.

> Jelly shoes – the original brand is called Sun Jellies and is still available today – were developed in France in 1946 by Monsieur Jean Dauphant. They are a classic fisherman shoe design, but it's reported Dauphant had the idea to make them out of rubber after World War II when there was a leather shortage in Europe. They've recently come back into fashion having made their way onto the catwalks of London designers Clements Ribeiro and Simone Rocha, although I'm still wearing mine in the sea.

Sun Jellies

Jellies

Jesus sandals

When I say Jesus sandals, I just mean very traditional-looking leather sandals, and when I say traditional, what I really mean is ancient – these shoes date back at least 10,000 years. Worn by the ancient Greeks, Egyptians and Romans, their success lies in their comfort and simplicity. It doesn't require a lot of leather to make a pair of sandals, so they have remained popular throughout history and with all sorts of people, regardless of status or wealth.

One of my favourite brands is Ancient Greek Sandals, whose simple leather sandals (made in Greece, obviously) have become a massive hit since their launch in 2012. I also love Havva for unusual yet classic styles.

Havva 'Athena' sandals

Mr Brogue played guitar in a band at school called Cover Your Ears Noddy, It's The Mary Janes (how they never made it big with a catchy name like that I will never know). They had no idea that they were referencing these simple shoes, mostly worn by children. I bet you all had a pair of school shoes that looked like this, with one simple, practical strap across the top of the foot. And they were probably from Start-Rite (mine were).

With a round toe Mary Janes look very Prince William circa 1985, so I'm only really keen on women wearing them if the shoe has a pointed toe. Designers like Miu Miu, Marc Jacobs and Tabitha Simmons have produced beautiful examples of these in recent years; they make a brilliant dress shoe for when everyone else will be wearing heels (FOOLS!).

Marc Jacobs Mary Janes

Mary Janes

Converse All Stars

The Converse Rubber Shoe company was founded in 1908, and the All Star was created in 1917 for basketball players. In 1921 a player called Charles 'Chuck' Taylor joined the team sponsored by Converse, and turned out to be a brilliant salesman too. Chuck worked with Converse to improve the shoe and before long they were being worn at the Olympics and by soldiers in training during World War II, before being absorbed into all areas of popular culture you can think of.

> What I love about Converse is that they are worn by everyone. You all have a pair, right? They hold a special place in my heart as they were the first pair of shoes I ever really wanted. NEEDED. I still have my first pair, bought for me on my thirteenth birthday after a lengthy search for some in just the right shade of purple (it was called 'grape').

From Kurt Cobain, to Rihanna, to Paul McCartney, they never fail to look cool when attached to someone holding a guitar or a microphone, no matter what the decade or fashion of the time. I hope I'll still be wearing my grape pair – yes, I still have them – when I'm old and grey. Well, purple does look brilliant with silver hair!

Moccasins

There's a lovely simplicity about moccasins; you can see exactly how the shoe is constructed. It's just two pieces of leather, joined together with a massive blanket stitch that gives the finished article the look of a very stylish Cornish pasty. Historically, they are the shoes that native Americans wore (and still wear), and are often decorated with fringing or beads, or even hand-painted scenes depicting nature.

> As well as the traditional styles that are still widely available, you can see evidence of moccasins on other shoes like deck shoes, loafers and Wallabees. I love this pair by Clarks, with their crêpe sole and fold-over detail; a totally modern way to wear this most ancient of shoe styles.

Clarks 'Tyler' boots

Monk shoes are a lovely alternative to a lace-up if you want to look a bit different from the pack. They generally come with either one buckle (monk) or two buckles (double monk) and are particularly lovely when decorated with broguing.

So what's the history behind these shoes? The clue's in the name. This style was popular with European monks who fancied a bit more protection than the sandals they commonly wore, but the convenience of a slip-on (the buckles usually have elastic for ease). Turns out monks are too busy to tie their laces! I prefer to wear mine with a snazzy pair of socks and turned-up jeans rather than a monk's habit, or, if they're a summery white pair like these, nothing works better than a flash of bare ankle.

Northern Cobbler 'Squawfish' double monk

Monk shoes

Oxfords

Oxfords (also known as 'Balmorals' in Scotland, 'Bals' in the USA and 'Richelieu' in France) are, unsurprisingly, called this because they were popular at Oxford University in the 1800s. You might be surprised to learn, though, that this very classic shoe has its roots in rebellion. They derive from a boot called an 'Oxonian' that eventually morphed into a lace-up shoe when students decided they didn't want to wear the dress code of the time any more: ankle boots.

> Often confused with Derbys, Oxfords are best described as having a closed front. The leather tabs with the lace holes are stitched under the vamp (the front section of the shoe) rather than on top. This means you can't open them as wide as a Derby; they feel a little more formal, and take a fair bit of wearing in.

Russell & Bromley 'Abacrombie' Oxfords

Over-knee boots

Tall boots can look a bit raunchy, particularly if they come up over the knee, but you can absolutely get away with wearing them and looking chic if they are flat. Not only that, they're a really practical option for keeping warm in the winter. I have a pair that are sheepskin lined all the way to the toe, and I'm yet to find a more stylish way of keeping snuggly and warm.

How you wear your tall boots is key though; my preferred style is over a pair of skinny jeans with either a long shirt or a baggy jumper. I'd advise a thick pair of deeply unsexy ribbed tights if you're going to dare to wear them with a short skirt, else it could all get a bit Julia Roberts in *Pretty Woman* before the make-over. Not a good look.

DUO boots

In the 1930s, a company called G.H. Bass Shoe Company began to produce shoes called 'Weejans', inspired by the slip-on shoes worn by Norwegian farmers. The story goes that the idea for the detail on the strap of the Weejan loafer came from Mr Bass's wife, who would give him a kiss on the cheek every day when he left for work (it's meant to look like a perfect lipstick stain).

Coincidentally, this 'slot' in the leather was also the perfect size to fit a penny into, which people often did back in 1930s America – one in each shoe. It was just enough money to make an emergency call in the newly introduced phone booths of the time, giving the Weejan its new (and far more sophisticated) name: the penny loafer.

Hobbs NW3 penny loafers

Penny loafers

Dr Martens boots

The air-cushioned soles that Damon Albarn buys
on the Portobello Road in Blur's 1993 song 'Blue Jeans'
were attached to a pair of Dr Martens boots. This
was around the same time I bought my first pair of
cherry reds, which I wore initially because of Nirvana
and grunge, but later adapted to Blur's sartorial nod
to suedeheads, pairing them with skinny turned-up
jeans and a Fred Perry polo shirt. In fact, it was this
exact outfit that got me refused entry into Harrods
when I was seventeen, though it was the small rip in
my jeans that was the offending detail rather than my
bovver boots.

> Anyway, that sounds like a lot of music genres, doesn't
> it? But what other shoe can say that it was adopted by
> everyone from goths and punks to mods and skin-
> heads, as well as the policemen that were called in to
> break up the fights between them. Although they went
> on to be associated with violence, DMs were originally
> a bigger hit with the fairer sex back in the 1940s when
> a German doctor designed them; 80 per cent were sold
> to women over the age of 40 during the first ten years
> of production.

One of your first pairs of shoes was probably a pair of plimsolls. You know, those ugly black slip-ons you had to wear for P.E. at school? Developed in the 1830s as a form of beachwear, their name derives from the Plimsoll line on a ship's hull – the point where the ship hits the water – and refers to the fact that if you get the canvas part of your plimsolls wet, your feet will get wet too (we've all learnt the hard way that Converse aren't ideal footwear for the rain!).

> I love their regional variations: 'gutties' in Northern Ireland, 'two boab sliders' in Scotland and 'daps' in the West Country. Whatever you call yours, I bet you've all got a pair lurking in your wardrobe. A real can't-live-without shoe.

Penelope Chilvers 'Sunshine' plimsolls

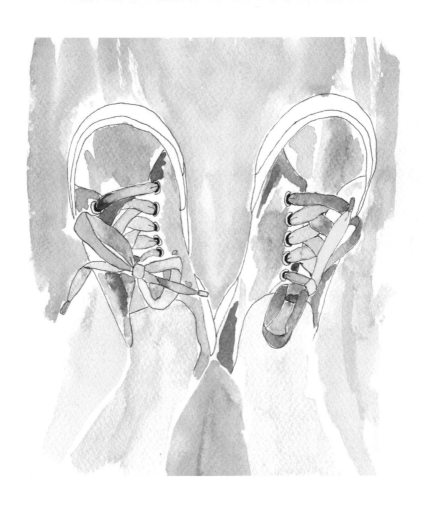

Plimsolls

These are my go-to smart shoe for posh dos, job interviews and a touch of sixties chic, and were a massive breakthrough in my quest to never wear heels. When I first decided to ditch the platforms, it was weddings and important meetings at work when I really struggled to find appropriate footwear. There's something about the pointy pump, though, that feels a little bit like a heel. Stiletto heels have been cited as having phallic substitute qualities – in other words, having something about them that makes a woman feel as powerful as an alpha male – and that sharp toe mimics the same idea.

Psychology aside, there's nothing more empowering than feeling comfortable, being able to run away from stuff and not falling down the stairs, which is a much better reason for choosing pointy flat pumps over heels.

Office pointy pumps

Pointy pumps

Pool slides

There's no mystery whatsoever to pool slides:
they are shoes that are easy to slide your foot in and
out of when you are by the pool. Simple. The real
mystery is how they have become such a fashion
favourite, with Nike and adidas versions popping up
in expensive magazine shoots. You can blame a
designer called Christopher Kane, who paraded jewel
embellished pool slides down the catwalk at London
Fashion Week in 2012, causing the fashion world to
fall into a state of lust.

> Slides have either one wide strap or two thinner straps
> that criss-cross over the middle of the foot and are
> usually made of plastic (it's waterproof, see?). This pair,
> though, are made of leather, so I won't be wearing them
> down at Lewisham Leisure Centre any time soon.

Ancient Greek Sandals 'Thais' leather slides

Saddle shoes are a lace-up shoe (usually an Oxford style) with a contrasting saddle-shaped panel of colour across the middle of the shoe. They were originally developed as a sports shoe in the early twentieth century, and were particularly popular for golfing because of their gripping rubber sole.

Of course, they were adopted by a stream of popular culture – as all interesting styles of shoe are – and saddle shoes became the footwear of choice for Lindy Hop and swing dancers in the 1940s; they loved them because they were so comfortable. Typically, girls would team them with a poodle skirt and ankle socks, but I also love them paired with very wide, slightly cropped jeans.

Vintage saddle shoes

Saddle shoes

Safari boots

I'm not sure that anyone other than Penelope Chilvers (one of my favourite brands!) makes safari boots, but I love them. They have the lower-cut ankle and crêpe sole of a desert boot, combined with the easy elastic sides you'll find on a Chelsea boot. If you ask me, that's the perfect hybrid.

> What I love about Penelope's boots is that she plays with the elastic itself to give the shoes a modern look. Some have a neon gusset; on other styles it's stripy. That crêpe sole is pretty much as comfortable as it gets, and the low cut on the ankle means you can wear them with skirts, even if you have short legs like me.

Penelope Chilvers safari boots

Nike Air Max

Nike was using its Air Cushioning Technology as early as 1979, but it wasn't until 1987 that the air bubble was exposed and the iconic Air Max was born. Designed by Tinker Hatfield (cool name!), an architect-turned-trainer-designer, they were reportedly inspired by Paris's Pompidou Centre; its inner workings totally visible from the outside of the building, just like the Air Max.

There are loads of versions of the Nike Air Max, including the ever-popular Air Max 90 and the Air Max 95, the names of which reflect the years they were first issued and the decade they were in their height of popularity: the nineties. My first pair were the Air Max 95 in orange, and only recently succumbed to the great shoe shop in the sky, despite my dad's best efforts to fix them with super glue. Liberty regularly collaborates with Nike to produce trainers with its iconic floral prints. I mean to pick myself up a pair every year, and every year they sell out before I get the chance. If you can't own them, I say, paint them…

There are some sheepskin boots on the market that I'm not very fond of: those big, chunky boots that were never meant to be worn as an outdoor shoe. A friend from New Zealand finds it hilarious that women in the UK wear them shopping or down the pub. I admit, I do own a pair and I love them as slippers, but I wouldn't be seen dead in them outside my house, other than to put the bins out on a Wednesday night.

Luckily, though, these are not the only style of sheepskin boot available. If you look for something with a proper Goodyear sole and a more elegant shape, they're brilliantly practical for the winter months. Beware of boots that aren't lined all the way to the end of the foot – you'll only end up with cold toes.

UGG 'Blayre' boots

Sheepskin boots

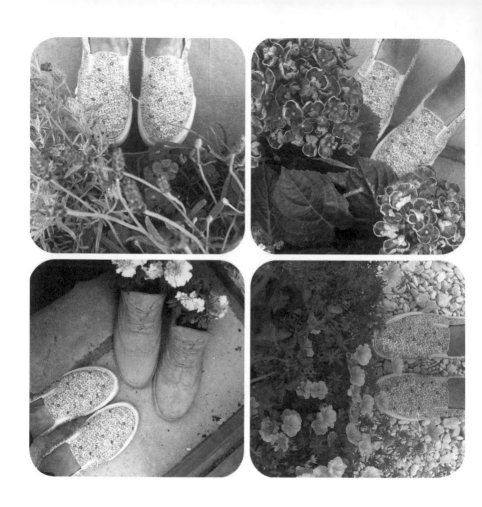

Skate shoes

As a teenager, I spent quite a bit of time hanging out with skateboarders, and shoes were very important to these guys. Brands like Vans and DC Shoes were the first to develop trainers specifically for the sport that included features like triple stitching (to make them more hardy – they take quite a battering) and special inner padding to help prevent foot injuries when landing a trick.

Of course, the lads I was friends with weren't wearing shoes like this with a pretty Liberty print! In fashion, the term 'skate shoe' has come to simply mean a slip-on trainer with elasticated inserts, and has gained popularity in recent years thanks to designer versions appearing on the catwalk. With the exception of Vans, don't expect your fashion trainers to cushion your feet when landing an Ollie...

Y.M.C. Liberty print shoes

Until recently, this style was more commonly known as a Venetian loafer, but I think the name smoking slipper better describes their luxurious feel. Often made of velvet with personalised motifs on the vamp, they have a bit of Hugh Hefner about them. In a totally good way – all money and silk dressing gowns!

I prefer them to ballet pumps because they are a more substantial shoe (they usually have a thicker sole) and the shape is just that bit more cool. I'll choose them over loafers because of the softer material and slightly more feminine shape. In fact, I like them so much I designed a pair myself – these ones are a collaboration between En Brogue and Jemima Vine.

En Brogue x Jemima Vine Edie slippers

Smoking slippers

T-bars

My earliest pair of T-bars were Clarks sandals and I was about two. My mum would buy them for me every summer, but would remove the T-bar strap in the middle so I didn't get a tan line on my foot. So thoughtful! How could she tell at such a young age that I would be into foot aesthetics…?

The Clarks sandals would have had a thick strap, but a skinny T-bar strap is far more elegant, whether it's on an enclosed shoe or a chic sandal like this. Does it make the ankle look more slender? A small foot like mine look a little longer? I've really no idea, I just know that my T-bar shoes get a higher number of compliments than any other style in my collection.

Marni sandals

These handsome slippers are more dapper than
their more formal counterparts – penny loafers –
and, with their dandy tassels on the toe, are for the
more flamboyant loafer-lovers amongst you.

> Best worn like a stylish Italian man with turned-up
> chinos and bare ankles, or take inspiration from Alexa
> Chung and team with a preppy mini-kilt, buttoned-up
> blouse and satchel slung across one shoulder. Of course
> the joy of a loafer is the lack of laces, which makes
> them the perfect smart shoe alternative to Derbys or
> Oxfords if you're feeling lazy.

Fratelli Rossetti loafers

Tassel loafers

Salt-Water sandals

There was a leather shortage after World War II, which meant that anyone producing shoes had to be imaginative. Walter Hoy – founder of Salt-Water sandals – was a cobbler who thought outside the box, with brilliant results. He began producing children's sandals in St. Louis, USA from the scraps of leather left over from making military boots and, seventy years on, they're as popular as ever, with the adult styles being worn by everyone from Sienna Miller to Florence Welch.

What's really great about Salt-Water sandals is that even though they are made of leather, they are totally waterproof. The leather is coated with a water resistant sealant, the buckles are rust-proof, and the soles are rubber – perfect for gripping on slippery surfaces. I've worn mine to swim off stony beaches, to fish for mackerel in a tiny boat, and just generally out and about in the 'Great' British summertime. I've also seen someone wearing them at a wedding (she looked great). And you can even stick them in the washing machine. Genius.

Trainers

The idea of adding rubber soles to sports shoes came from South American Indians, who applied latex from rubber trees to their feet for protection. It's a tricky material, but a chap called Charles Goodyear (he who the tyres are named after) discovered the vulcanisation process in 1839 – put simply, it turns natural rubber into a more durable material – which changed the shoe industry forever.

Trainers first made their way out of the sports hall in the 1930s, but it wasn't until the 1980s that they really came into their own with the rise of Hip Hop culture. They were certainly the starting point for my shoe obsession, and I have been known to sleep with a new pair next to my bed so they're the first thing I see when I wake up...

Hannah in New Balance
Mr Brogue in Nike

While I do like a good long walk, I'm not suggesting that you actually go for a hike in these boots, merely that you appreciate the aesthetic of a practical, sturdy lace-up. I really love a contrasting shoe lace, and that's a key part of this particular pair – a bold colour like green, yellow or orange works equally well, particularly if they are flecked with black and the lace is nice and chunky.

Another key feature is the boot lace hooks, in place of holes, towards the top of the ankle. Obviously these are for practicality, but they make a really nice design feature too.

Penelope Chilvers 'Atlas' boots

Walking boots

Wellington boots

Imagine having a boot named after you and two hundred years later, it's still totally en vogue. That's exactly what happened to the Duke of Wellington, who had no idea when he asked his shoemaker to construct a sturdy knee-high boot that in the 21st century, hundreds of thousands of girls at festivals around the world would still be wearing his namesake design, only now with tiny denim shorts instead of his preferred attire, jodhpurs.

Of course the Duke's wellies were made of leather, though it was as early as 1853 that they began to be made of rubber by Aigle, a company that still makes lovely Wellington boots today. This pair are by Hunter though, a wellie boot brand so successful that it recently started showing on the catwalk at London Fashion Week.

Hunter + Rag & Bone boots

Wing tips

Another confusing lace-up entry to baffle you with now. Wing tips are shoes with a particular type of design on the toe – where the cut of the leather sort of looks like the shape of a very basic drawing of a seagull. I've chosen a block coloured pair here to really demonstrate it clearly; the dark brown bit at the front is the wing tip.

Wing tips are often used on Derbys, Oxfords or Monks, and more often than not incorporate broguing too. I love them; my brogues just wouldn't feel the same without them. They even look great on informal shoes too, like trainers.

Grenson 'Rose' brogues

I think this might be my favourite shoe name, not least because I love winkles. They get their name from the exaggerated pointy toe, which was likened to the pin used to extract winkles from their shells. Yummy.

Also known as 'pikes', they first became popular in the sixties and have always had a strong association with rock 'n' roll. In the noughties you could expect to see musicians such as Jack White and the Kings of Leon wearing them, although some of my favourites were the hilarious comedy versions worn by Vic Reeves and Bob Mortimer in the 1990s.

Antipodium X ASOS shoes

Winkle pickers

Superga sneakers

These tennis shoes have been around for over 100 years; they were first made in Italy by Walter Martiny in 1911. Although they have been a favourite with Italians all that time, it's only in recent years that they've enjoyed mass popularity around the world. As well as collaborations with Mary-Kate and Ashley Olsen's fashion line The Row, Brit designer Henry Holland and high fashion label Versace, it was a centennial UK campaign in 2011 with Alexa Chung that really brought these humble little sneakers into high fashion and the mainstream.

> The most famous (and my favourite) style is the 2750 shoe, which was first produced in 1925, and hasn't changed a jot since. It might have a less catchy name than its tennis shoe contemporary – the adidas Stan Smith – but I love its simplicity and that Italian chic really shines through. Although it looks great in bright colours and prints, you really can't beat it in classic white, navy or red.

Shoe Cleaning, Care and Tips

Wearing shoes in

If you're buying a pair of really well-made leather shoes, they might take a bit of wearing in, but it's usually worth the perseverance. I only have one (very expensive) pair of shoes that have, in spite of my best efforts, been relegated to just looking pretty on my shoe shelves. With masculine shoes like Oxfords and monks, I'd advise your first few wears to include socks; never risk a bare foot on the first day. If they feel particularly stiff, you can try softening them up by warming the inside of the shoe with a hair dryer and wearing them around the house with a thick pair of socks.

I tend to always carry plasters in my bag, just in case, too. Sometimes a pair of shoes you've had for years will suddenly start to rub because it's a really hot day or you've walked a bit too far in them. For heels, you can't beat Compead blister plasters (they're transparent too), and for smaller foot areas, only a fabric plaster will do, as anything else tends to slip off.

Cleaning

Unfortunately, it's only really canvas shoes like Converse that you can stick in the washing machine when they get a bit grubby. Prevention is key with suede and pale-coloured leather; I swear by Clarks' protective spray as it's cheap and it works. You'll then just need to spruce them up with a suede brush if you get caught in the rain. Shoes with a trendy white sole and white leather trainers come up good as new with a bit of kitchen cleaner (must include bleach) and some elbow grease. Your cleaning kit should also include a brush (for muddy soles) and a neutral polish for leather (no need to buy all the different colours).

Storage

How you store your shoes can affect their shape; if you just bung them in a pile at the back of your wardrobe, don't expect them to look good when they come out. I'm lucky enough to have space for shoe shelves (built by Mr Brogue) but you can always line them up in pairs under the bed.

Soft leather shoes can lose their shape, so I like to use shoe trees. These ones are vintage – you can pick them up cheaply on eBay or at car boot sales. If your shoes come with dust bags, keep them to use when packing for a holiday. Packing your socks inside your shoes is also a good idea to prevent your shoes getting squashed (and saves space, too!).

Shoe Spotting

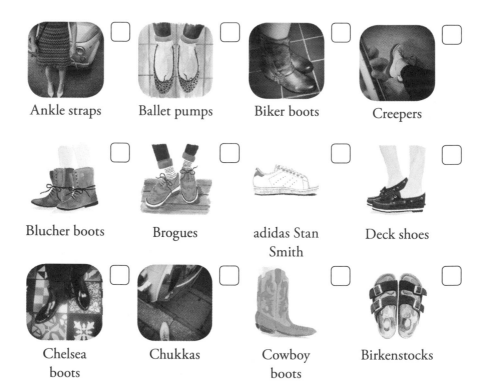

Ankle straps

Ballet pumps

Biker boots

Creepers

Blucher boots

Brogues

adidas Stan Smith

Deck shoes

Chelsea boots

Chukkas

Cowboy boots

Birkenstocks

Are you a bit of a shoe gazer?

Tick off these styles as you see them (or even as you buy them if you're a shoe hoarder, like me!) in my handy shoe spotting guide.

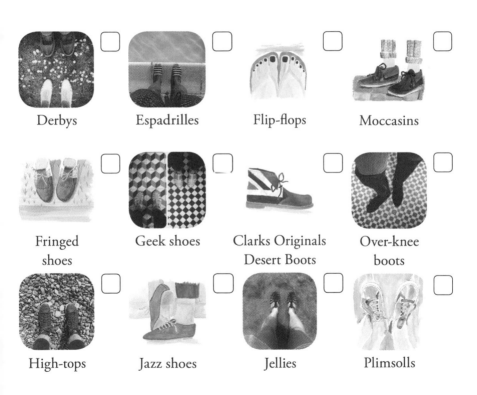

Derbys

Espadrilles

Flip-flops

Moccasins

Fringed shoes

Geek shoes

Clarks Originals Desert Boots

Over-knee boots

High-tops

Jazz shoes

Jellies

Plimsolls

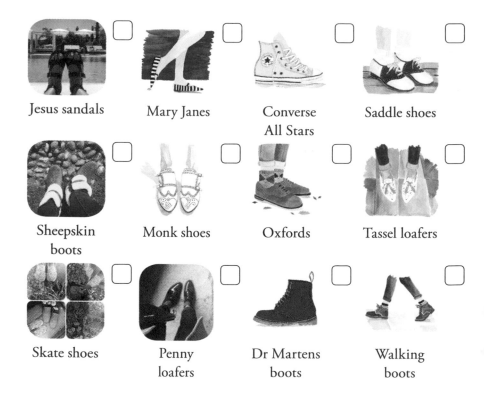

Jesus sandals ☐

Mary Janes ☐

Converse All Stars ☐

Saddle shoes ☐

Sheepskin boots ☐

Monk shoes ☐

Oxfords ☐

Tassel loafers ☐

Skate shoes ☐

Penny loafers ☐

Dr Martens boots ☐

Walking boots ☐

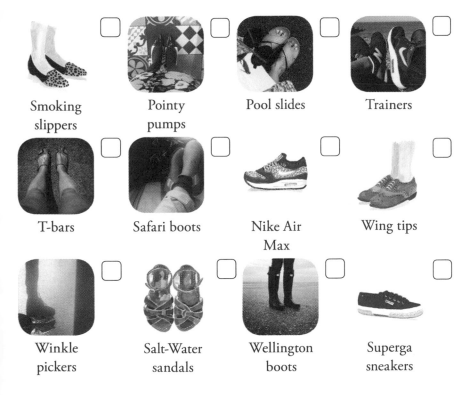

Smoking slippers

Pointy pumps

Pool slides

Trainers

T-bars

Safari boots

Nike Air Max

Wing tips

Winkle pickers

Salt-Water sandals

Wellington boots

Superga sneakers

Styling Tips

How to wear Bermuda shorts

Bermudas are great if you like your legs
from the knees down but aren't so keen
on your thighs. I spend a lot of time on
the beach, so I like this laid-back look, but
tailored versions also look great for work
in the summer.

*shorts, by Topshop Boutique; sandals, by
Birkenstock*

What to wear as a wedding guest

People often lose their style mojo at
weddings – why wear kitten heels and a
shift dress if you never ordinarily would?
I wore this outfit to my brother's wedding,
complete with matching printed top, and
felt totally 'me'.

*trousers, by Bimba Y Lola; monk shoes, by
Northern Cobbler*

How to wear skate shoes

I like to mix my sports shoes with
something smart to avoid looking like
I might actually be on my way to the gym,
so I pair my skate shoes with tailored
trousers. I also like to wear running shoes
with pencil skirts.

trousers, H&M; skate shoes, Essentiel
Antwerp

What to wear to the office

Leopard print flats are a great workwear
investment because you can wear them
at the weekends with jeans, too. A pointy
pair like this works with a pencil or an
A-line; whatever suits you best.

skirt, by Baukjen; smoking slippers, by
Russell & Bromley

How to wear ankle boots with bare legs
It's all about the height of the boot
compared with the length of your legs.
As I'm quite short, I need a really low boot
to get the proportions right, as well as
quite a lot of leg on show. If you're tall, try
a longer hem with a taller boot.
*shorts, vintage; Desert Boots, by Penelope
Chilvers*

How to wear flats as a bridesmaid
This is what I wore when I was bridesmaid
for my friend Daisy. The other two bridesmaids were very tall and wore heels and
even though Mr Brogue mistook me for a
child when I walked down the aisle with
them, I was really happy with this outfit.
*dress, by Marilyn Moore; pumps,
by Diane von Furstenberg*

How to do turn-ups

Turn-ups really help when wearing flat shoes. A flash of ankle – or when you're wearing ankle boots, shin – helps to elongate your legs a little bit. Suddenly the length of your jeans becomes vital; mine are usually slightly cropped or turned up twice.

IDA cords, by Donna Ida; safari boots, by Penelope Chilvers

How to wear socks

Of course, you can't flash bare ankles when it's cold, so invest in a few pairs of really nice socks. I love spotty designs, or a classic Argyle pair like this. Turn your jeans up once to really show them off.

jeans, by MiH Jeans; penny loafers, by Hobbs NW3

Shoe Shopping Directory

best for not spending a fortune
& Other Stories (stories.com)
Bimba Y Lola (bimbaylola.com)
Clarks (clarks.co.uk)
Dune (dunelondon.com)
Hudson (hudsonshoes.com)
Office (office.co.uk)
Schuh (schuh.co.uk)
TOMs (toms.co.uk)
Topshop (topshop.com)
Zara (zara.com)

best for sporty styles
adidas (adidas.co.uk)
Bata (bata.com)
Converse (converse.com)
Crooked Tongues (crookedtongues.com)
Essential Antwerp (essential-antwerp.com/en)
Feit (feitdirect.com)
Fred Perry (fredperry.com)

Inkkas (inkkas.com)
Nike (nike.com)
New Balance (newbalance.co.uk)
OLI13 (oli13.com)
Size? (size.co.uk)
Superga (superga.co.uk)
Vagabond (vagabond.com)
Vans (vans.co.uk)
Veja (veja-store.com)
Walsh (normanwalshuk.com)

best for sandals

Ancient Greek Sandals (ancient-greek-sandals.com)
Birkenstock (birkenstock.co.uk)
By Larin (bylarin.com)
Gandys (gandysflipflops.com)
Havaianas (havaianas-store.com)
Havva (havvamustafa.com)
La Paire (lapaire.co.uk)
Salt-Water (salt-watersandals.com)
Sun Jellies (sunjellies.com)

best for lots of brands in one place

Anthropologie (anthropologie.eu)
ASOS (asos.com)
Atterley Road (atterleyroad.com)
Bicester Village (bicestervillage.com)

Harvey Nichols (harveynichols.com)
My Wardrobe (my-wardrobe.com)
Selfridges (selfridges.com)
Shoescribe (shoescribe.com)
The Outnet (theoutnet.com)
Urban Outfitters (urbanoutfitters.com/UK)
Yoox (yoox.com)

best for smart shoes

Church's (church-footwear.com)
French Sole (frenchsole.com)
Hobbs NW3 (hobbs.co.uk)
Jemima Vine (jemimavine.co.uk)
Kurt Geiger (kurtgeiger.com)
L.K. Bennett (lkbennett.com)
Lucy Choi (lucychoilondon.com)
Paul Smith (paulsmith.co.uk)
Pretty Ballerinas (prettyballerinas.com)
Russell & Bromley (russellandbromley.co.uk)

best for boots

Celtic & Co (celticandco.co.uk)
Cobra Society (thecobrasociety.com)
DUO (duoboots.com)
Dr Martens (drmartens.com/UK)
Hunter (hunter-boot.com)
Ilse Jacobsen (ilse-jacobsen.nl)

Palladium (palladiumboots.co.uk)
Steve Madden (stevemadden.com)
Timberland (timberlandonline.co.uk)
UGG (uggaustralia.co.uk)

best for showstoppers

Grenson (grenson.co.uk)
Folk (folkclothing.com)
Marni (marni.com)
Nicholas Kirkwood (nicholaskirkwood.com)
Penelope Chilvers (penelopechilvers.com)
Pollini (pollini.com)
Rupert Sanderson (rupertsanderson.com)
Tabitha Simmons (tabithasimmons.com)
Toast (toast.co.uk)
Y.M.C. (youmustcreate.com)

best niche brands

Chatelles (mychatelles.com)
Chie Mihara (chiestore.com)
F-Troupe (f-troupe.com)
Labour of Love (labour-of-love.co.uk)
Northern Cobbler (northerncobbler.com)
Seven Boot Lane (sevenbootlane.com)
Swear (swear-london.com)
The Jacksons (thejacksons.co.uk)
Zoe Lee (zoelee.co.uk)

Acknowledgements

There are so many people to thank for this book, but I'll start with Mr Brogue – otherwise known as my husband, Mark Rochell – not least because you put up with my vast shoe collection and redecorated our bedroom to accommodate it. You're my biggest fan and my most honest critic (which is just as important) and I couldn't have done this without you.

Thanks to Mum and Dad for your constant support and also for having the genes that blessed me with photogenic feet. I never knew until recently how important that would be! To my brother Joe and sister-in-law Zoe for your advice and help, to Holly Jolliffe for your fantastic photographic skills, and to my dear friends and family for spreading the En Brogue love. I wish I could name you all individually but there isn't space, and that makes me a very lucky person indeed.

Special thanks to Elizabeth Hallett and Kate Miles for seeing the En Brogue potential and understanding what I wanted to do, and Alice Laurent, Lyndsey Ng and all at Saltyard for producing my dream book in such a short space of time.

Lastly, and most importantly, to all the readers of EnBrogue.com – this book wouldn't exist without your enthusiastic love for flat shoes. I can't thank you all enough for reading, sharing and joining in. You have been brilliant and this book is for you, so I hope you enjoy reading it as much as I have enjoyed writing it.

First published in Great Britain in 2014 by Saltyard Books
An imprint of Hodder & Stoughton
An Hachette UK company

1

A CIP catalogue record for this title is available from the British Library.

ISBN 978 1 473 60650 0
eBook ISBN 978 1 473 60651 7

Book design by Aka Alice
Typeset in Adobe Garamond Pro

Proof reader Annie Lee

Printed and bound in Italy by L.E.G.O. Spa

Hodder & Stoughton policy is to use papers that are natural, renewable and recyclable products and made from wood grown in sustainable forests. The logging and manufacturing processes are expected to conform to the environmental regulations of the country of origin.

Saltyard Books
338 Euston Road
London NW1 3BH

www.saltyardbooks.co.uk

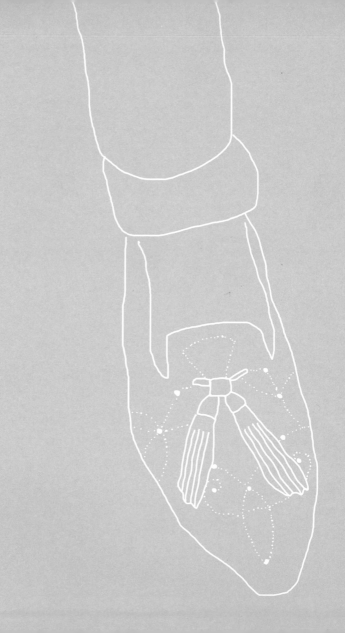